N●CTURNAL

wilder

also by wilder

wild is she

Andrews McMeel
PUBLISHING®

NOCTURNAL

i am an open window.
tangled sheets at 1am.
i count stars instead of sheep
and dream with my eyes open.
it's how i know that i'll always
remember them.

i talk to the moon and she listens—
a little louder than anyone else has.
and in those moments when my
voice only knows how to be silent,
i write her letters while the rest of
the world is sleeping.

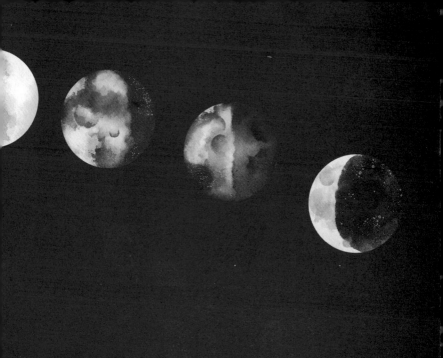

i hope she finds them
one day.

for sam

DUSK

i climb mountains to see the world
wear different shades of honesty.

and isn't it beautiful
the way we see things change?
the way our eyes fall in love
with a different time of day
knowing that it will never hurt
when tomorrow comes.

my eyes will remember
how to love the world
under changing skies.

when the light changes,
so does the view.

∴

just as the sun met the horizon,
i came into this world
with eyelids that looked like
a bruise-coloured sky.

my skin knew the taste of salt
before i could meet the ocean,
but as my gentle screams filled the room
to let you know that i could breathe,
i learned what it felt like
to be saved while drowning.

i've always been told that
i was born chasing sunsets, but
sometimes i wonder if i'm really
just trying to find a way
to be in two places at once.

there is something graceful
about the way time passes by—
how it gives itself away,
never knowing whose hands
will stop to hold it before
it leaves.

i found you
in all of the things
you left behind,
like love letters
folded in dressers
and shadows on the
bedroom floor.

i have wept
for beautiful things,
raising flowers with my rain.

i brake for birds
that aren't ready to
fly upward
and carry spiders
to new homes.

and i am learning how to
be this gentle with my own skin.

—chloë

this is how i pour myself
into all of the spaces
i never knew i could fit,
like a sun that finds
the smallest corners through
fingerprinted glass.

it isn't always graceful,
but *becoming* never is.

i'm still trying
to find the parts of me
i left hidden
between pages
of a story i never
wanted to forget,
but you were always
in the last place
i looked.

we found forgiveness
on the edge of
tomorrow and falling.

i am waiting
to catch my breath

and you

you were showing
me how to save
myself.

and what a beautiful thing it is,
being made to hold on or
let go.

—*hands*

i will leave my daydreams out
for anyone to find
and spread them like seeds—
waiting for the wind to carry them
to safer ground.

i will love them from a distance
    until they grow in my direction.

i will look up and reach
    for what has always been mine.

i hide
behind closed blinds
during daylight
and bury my skin
under blankets that
know me better
than i do.

i hope someday
the light will find a way
through the cracks
while i stand from
the outside looking in
so i can tell her,

i love you
and i always will.

—self-love

one day i will
remember
this bravery—
this storm beneath
my skin.

you couldn't see me,
but you knew i was coming.

these skies
will teach you patience.
the unwavering kind that
keeps your feet on the
ground while the rest of
the world feels unsteady.

she will fall for miles.
land on your face,
your shoulders,
your hands

and as her colours change,
i see how unafraid you are
of those that don't know
whether they are coming
or going.

i still can't tell
which one of you
is the miracle.

i hold promises
between my lips
hoping to speak them
to someone
who will show me
what it's like to be
held with more
than just two hands.

∴

my eyes have looked
through rose-tinted glass all my life
and i will never lose sight of a horizon
that knows how to see me
even when everything else
is falling.

i will visit you at sunset.
find you in all of the places
you thought i would never look.
park bench. oak tree. bookstore.
i will read you a story.
listen to your favorite song on the radio.
i will remember this moment in pictures.
black and white,
like coffee.
i will wait at the corner of
i miss you and sorry.
wave in your direction,
hoping you will notice me
while i try to remember if this is
hello or goodbye.

a heart was made
to live in the dark;

maybe we were, too.

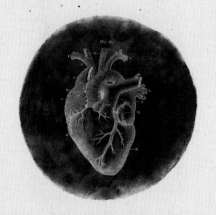

this is the part
where i put myself
back together.
this is the part
where i tell you
i'm okay and hope
you won't notice
that i am already
ripping at the seams,
grasping at straws
that have always
been out of reach.

i haven't met a cloud
that didn't touch me—
changing shapes in the wind;
not because we asked
her to be different, but
because the wild showed her
it was okay to be free.

and like the sun i am

spinning
                d i z z y

running after the moon,
trying to catch something
i can never have.

it's a hopeless thing,
this speaking your name
wondering if you will hear me.

—falling ~~on~~ for deaf ears

i cry with my eyes closed
so i can't see how bad it hurts.

everything breaks once, you said
but give anything time and it will heal
if you let it.

this was my first lesson of survival.

THEY TOLD ME TO

RUN LIKE

THE WIND

BUT I WAS THE ONE CREATING IT

someday
i will show
you what it feels
like to love
with your
eyes closed
and your
heart open.

today
i am learning
to do the same.

you loved me quietly,
like footprints in the snow.

(you were there and i wasn't expecting you.)

the seasons are changing,
but you still look the same.

i can hear the forest breathe—
the way it sighs when the air passes through.

like a song that never wants to end.
like a whisper that knows i will hear it
even though they never could.

i do not wish for tomorrow
because it brings me further away
from tonight.

it brings me further
        away
              from you.

the lights are fading behind me
in the rearview mirror
and it's raining again.

another goodbye that came too soon—
a broken city that hoped i would never leave.

i held on even though i knew heartbreak would come knocking at my door. it has always known where to find me, but i have never been very good at hiding.

and that was the difference between you and me—i handed you forever and you swept tomorrow under the rug hoping i would never know where to look.

maybe it's true that good-bye is never far away, because i left a key under the mat and i'm still waiting to see which one of you will use it first.

i am proof that some things
will never fit because this shirt
of yours will always feel like
a cape that hangs past my
knees and leaves me drowning.

*but this is what it feels like when love
is the hero of the story.*

i've been told i love more
than i can handle,
but the weight of emptiness
in my hands feels like a
flower that misses the rain
and i love the taste of
water too much to go hungry.

there are bruises all over my skin
and i'm still not sure where they came from,
but i love the colour of sunset
and healing will always look beautiful.

i will find you
in between dusk
and twilight.
i will balance you gently
on my fingers
and save you from
falling into glass jars.
i will set you free
knowing that their
eyes should see
how you hold on
to your own *light*.
i will watch you fade
into the trees and wait
until i find *mine*.

—*fireflies*

and when they ask me
are you afraid of the dark?
i will remind them that
there's nothing to fear
when the night is a reason
we can see how honest
everything shines
while the rest of the world
is hiding.

you are always enough

LIGHT

NORTHERN LIGHTS

they said i was *the greatest show on earth*
and watched me in the dark
with big eyes and curious hearts
hoping i would never end.
even though time has never been on my side
i'm starting to understand that maybe
love is blind, but a broken clock is still right
two times a day.

she showed me how to leave pieces
of my heart inside stories

       that kept me *steady*.
       that made me *feel* something.

i don't think there will ever be too many
wildflowers pressed against the spine,
or train ticket bookmarks waiting
for me to find my way back again.

there are some places
that know me better than i do—
a home that is never too far away.

*flowers take time to grow
and so do i*

these rivers run like they are
trying to find somewhere else
to call home.

maybe i'm just trying to do the same.

i planted seeds
beneath this skin
knowing the sun
would always come
back for me
even when nothing
else could.

this is how
i bury my wounds
under oceans.

my eyes may burn
just like the rest of me,
but i came here for healing
and the salt on my tongue
will always remind me
that everything stings
before it goes.

i found home
in this survival.

i held my own hand,
opened the window,
had a conversation
with the night,
and forgot every
reason there was
to hide.

BECOMING A SUNFLOWER

dig deep
face the sun
open your heart
catch the rain
stay wild
be messy
fall (*it won't hurt, i promise*)
keep breathing

NOTE TO SELF
even flowers are beautiful when it's dark.

we turn to the sky waiting for answers
never knowing that looking up
was all we'd ever need.

there is a dream to catch
and it's closer than you think.

THE SKY

IS HIGH

BUT MY HOPE

IS HIGHER.

there is a smile
inside of me waiting
to reach upward,
like a balloon that
wants to be free.

the flying may come to an end,
but the view reminds me
what i would've missed
if i had never let go.

−a new beginning

i see rainbows
with my eyes
and wonder why
they thought
chasing dreams was
all we had left.

∴

I DO NOT
LET THINGS GO SOFTLY.

EVEN THOUGH MY VOICE
IS HARD TO HEAR
THE WORDS STILL FALL
FROM MY MOUTH
LIKE A TREE
THAT KEEPS GIVING
UNTIL IT HAS
NOTHING LEFT.

I MAY BE
EMOTIONALLY NUDE,
BUT THE VIEW IS STILL
BEAUTIFUL.

i learned not to fear the falling.

even if i hit rock bottom,
the dust will settle
and my arms will still know
how to reach.

i carry hope in my pockets
like pennies that don't know
which way they will land.
but even if i find myself
on the wrong side of right,
my hands will show me
that there is always room
for change.

i can hold so much light
and darkness, too.

—conversations with the sky

this heart is a drum
in the marching band,
playing for a crowd
that wants to be heard.

it is standing room only
under a sky full of stars.
their eyes are open and
i am cheering from
the sidelines
reminding them that
love is loud even
when it's dark.

you can hear me and i can hear you.

I CLIMB ABOVE
SKYSCRAPERS
WITH EYES THAT
STILL REMEMBER HOW
TO SEE THE STARS
EVEN WHEN
THE SKY IS FULL
OF A CITY THAT
NEVER WANTS
TO SLEEP.

TIME IS

STANDING

STILL

AND I AM

WAITING FOR

SOMEONE

TO FIND ME.

how to handle me with care:

forgive;
then show me how
to do the same.

we screamed at the top of our
lungs through tunnels that looked
like they would never end. you
told me to hold on to my light,
like it was something you couldn't
live without (*and honestly neither
could i*). it was a simple love, the
kind where you spelled my name
right on the first try and i knew it
was meant to be.

i think i met you in a different
life. everything about you is
familiar, like a song i've heard
before. like the smell of rain on
my summer dress. like sunday
morning in bed. like yesterday.

i would remember your mess any-
where and i know i'm too much
of a disaster for you to forget.
we are the perfect storm. the
sky echoes and all we can do is
look up like there's something
we might miss.

like the sky, i'm always moving.

you didn't want me to leave,
but you never asked me to stay.

i kissed the book i gave you
with my favorite red lipstick
and hoped you would
hold on to it forever
like a pinky holds a promise.

that's the thing about me.
i'm always leaving pieces of myself behind
for others to keep and for once
i don't feel empty.

tea-stained paper
beneath these hands and a pen
that doesn't know how to work.
a poem will not write itself,
but what words are left
for someone that didn't
know how to stay?

this is a poem about somebody else.
this is a poem about someone who chose to stay.

dear self,

it was real because you felt it.
love is meant to hurt when it leaves.

I'M

LETTING GO

LIKE

OCTOBER

AND

MY EYES

FEEL LIKE

SPRING.

and it was like the wind.
i couldn't see it,
but it moved me.

–free spirit

i wrap my arms around change
hoping for a miracle.

the colours are fading,
i am falling,
but my voice doesn't shake
on the way down.

WHAT

KEEPS

YOU

AWAKE?

a heart that never stops

dreaming.

HOWL

silence isn't lonely.

—things the moon taught me

my toes dangle over dark edges bravely,
while my hands collect wishes that have
forgotten how to shine.

they ask
why did you save me?

the truth is,
i think we all want to be held
after we let go.

i think we all want to be saved.

I'M

LOSING

SLEEP

LIKE

THE ONE

THAT

GOT AWAY.

and i can't help
but wonder
where the night goes
after it says goodbye.

i think it left with you.

witness this unraveling.
this coming together
while falling apart.

i am two ends of a rope,
one held between fists
while the other lies
on the ground next to
blistered hands that
couldn't hold on.

i am scraped knees,
dirt under fingernails.

they say i've been defeated,
but i will always remember how
to smile when it hurts.

i've let myself
come undone
~~all at once~~ in pieces
and i'm still waiting
for my arms to learn
that i have always
been worth the weight,
no matter how many
scars my palms wear
from trying to hold
all of me together.

there is a part of me
that will always carry
almost inside the corners
of my heart.

i'm here.
i'm waiting.

these hands have
memorized
so many beautiful things.
even in the dark,
i always know where
to find you.

i found my heart
inside of a shoe box
next to pieces of you
holding pieces of me.
you were rough
around the edges
and i was too many words
written on folded paper,
hidden under photographs
that didn't remember what
it was like to feel the walls.

sometimes i wonder
how much longer i will need to wait
for you to lose your way
back to me.

sometimes i wonder
which one of us will find
you first.

—lost & found

and if the world stops,
all i want is a little more forever
with you.

i wear the word *wild*
with a body that has forgotten
how to be anything less.

there are no
regrets living here.
only storms waiting for
a name.

i felt you like
before the rain comes;

wind on my face,
the smell of something
that's about to change.

you were like a robber in the night.

taking what wasn't yours,
then running away,
praying i would never catch you.

you said i cried wolf
again and again
then called it desperation, but
maybe this is my way
of letting you know
that i'm here
whether you're coming
or not.

it is a soft landing;

a bird in the trees,
these tears on my pillow.

hold on to my limbs, you said. so i grabbed you
tightly between calloused hands that already
knew you by heart.

you should know that my skin cracks under
pressure and i bruise easily, but that will
never stop me from climbing above shades of
green to see the world through your eyes.

looking down at the forest floor, i am
reminded of the damage they have caused—
making homes out of you, never knowing
that you've always been enough.
and as i cry myself to sleep in the bend of
your knee, you remind me that all hearts take
time to grow.

maybe all along you've been the one
holding me.

—a heart held up by trees

i was the sea
and you were a
glass-bottomed
boat.

i asked you to jump,
but you looked at me from above
wanting to see how much more
i would give away.

i don't know if i can
keep showing you
my love.

i don't know if i can
keep waiting for you
to hear me.

in   a   not-so-distant   sky   i
overheard   the   moon   share
stories   with   the   clouds
about the way things change.

please don't cry when i go.
darkness is a familiar ghost
and i've been sleepwalking
for days, but dreams are loud
for a reason and this compass
has never been wrong before.

you told me that you
dream in colour.
that it was like you
could wrap your arms
around them and forget
what you left behind.

i know we live in different worlds,
but i promise, you do not need
to look very hard to find me—
maybe i'll remind you of all the
reasons you want to stay.

—*a star in your sky*

what an
impossible thing,
this taking a shot
in the dark
wondering where
i may land—
hoping your hands
will reach out
to catch me.

home has a way
of letting the most
beautiful people
hold your hand.

let me be thunder
and lightning.
unpredictable.
reckless.
with a voice that
echoes across the
darkened sky.

you watched me from a distance,
knowing that i was made to disappear.

i said goodbye, hoping i'd be back soon.

you keep hiding behind doors
that i don't know how to open.
i will knock.
i will wait for you to answer.
i will reach out with my fingers,
scratch them against the floor
hoping you will notice.

you told me that you were
running from the truth
and i would be lying if i said
i was doing the same.

some things are left unsaid
like stories resting on nightstands
waiting to be held again,
but i will always remember
the way you folded
me at my corners
like there was a part of me
you wanted to come back to.

when you wonder
how much love
i have left to give,
do not look
at my wreckage
with fear.
my hands love
the touch of survival
and my heart
has always known
how to build.

i have indigo eyes
and an atlas heart
that lives on the outside
of my chest, but i never
know where i'm going.
point me in the
right direction and
i promise, i will still
get lost.

*i've never wanted to follow
anyone's lead.*

i look through paned-glass
windows at midnight
and watch the moon
turn my skin wild—
it's the only thing
i will surrender to.

shadows stretch above my head
while my introverted heart
breaks the silence for a sky
that makes a voice feel honest.
and when you tell me that
you hear me, i hope you will
see how my eyes keep looking
in your direction.

i found you
and i don't want to let go.

—wolf

i've spent my life
looking for a place
to call mine, tucking myself
in at night wondering
what dreams will fall
out from under me.
they always tell me
there's no place like home,
but i'm still trying to find
somewhere to land.

NOW YOU SEE ME.
NOW YOU DON'T.

—*ghosted*

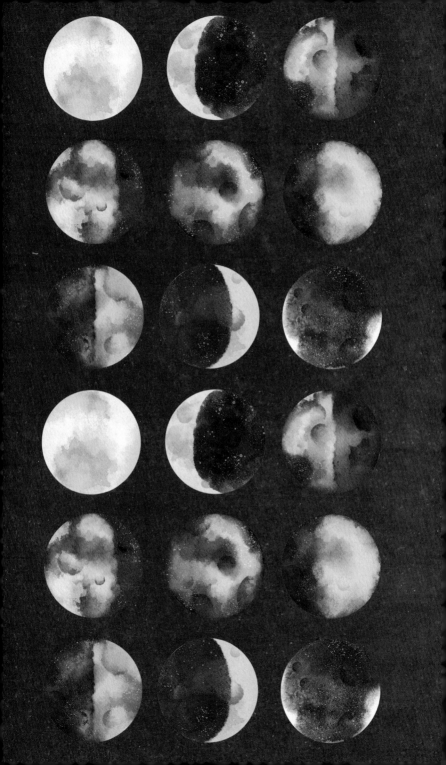

these roads have seen
more sadness than i know
how to carry.

do you feel the ache?
do you feel the weight?

from every goodbye that stretched for miles,
never knowing when it might return
for what it left behind.

THERE IS A FOG IN THE DISTANCE

they can't see me
and i can't either.

i am tired of chasing
things that want to leave.

—the sun, moon, and you

they strike matches
forgetting that our bodies
can take whole forests down.

don't play with fire
if you can't handle the flame.

.look closely
at this courage.
watch how it grows
through the cracks
under their feet.

celebrate
your survival.
find your arms
and hold on to hope,
knowing it is yours
to lose.

in the end,
you don't need
anyone else to
make you feel
alive.

i dream of an almighty night
full of wonder and a north. star
that knows the way.

there is a certain darkness that
lives above us as we watch
the night carry on with grace—
embracing a moon that wants
to hide away for a little longer
because it knows the sky
has something else to give.

—*new moon*

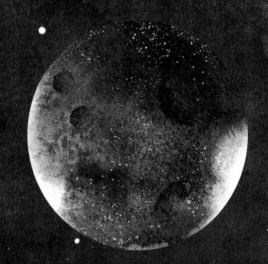

I AM NOT

WHERE YOU

LEFT ME.

I AM ALL

THE PLACES

I HAVE NEVER

BEEN.

ALL I WANTED WAS

SPACE

AND YOU TOLD ME

TO LOOK AT THE SKY

my body is in a deep sleep,
but my heart still feels the ache
and i'm waiting for a dream
to shake the rest of me awake.

i met a magician in my dreams.
his voice was honest and so were his
hands—it was beautiful the way he
held the world together with eyes the
colour of oceans.

they were reflective and forgiving in
all the ways someone like me needed
because i have carried the weight
of *i'm sorry* for so long that i almost
forget what it feels like to breathe
(*and not drown*).

he had a five o'clock shadow and a
pet hummingbird named *promise* that
sat on his pinky like she lived there
all her life. and when he reached
in my direction i thought maybe
he would hold me, too. instead he
walked with me to morning and said,

OPEN YOUR EYES.

THE BEST IS YET TO COME.

but a part of me will always wonder what it feels like to be held by someone that never wants you to leave.

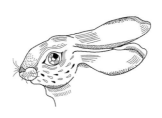

i wrote these words for you
in my dreams

LUCID DREAMS

you spoke to me in whispers.
wings against the windowsill,
shadows on the wall.
and as i held you between gentle fists,
i surrendered you to the night
knowing that a part of you
would never want to leave.

M O T H

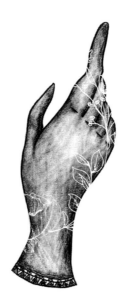

TO A FLAME

i saw the fire burning,
but i didn't think that you
would throw me in.

(your flag was red and mine was white.)

∴

maybe we forgot the words—
maybe we forgot how to say them.
but no matter the silence between us,
i will know where to look
in the middle of a crowded room.

E Y E S   W I D E

SHUT

there will always be things
closing behind me.

slamming doors,
mouths that had nothing left to say,
eyes that forgot how to find me.

and now i realize that some things
are worth ~~losing~~ leaving.

i lost you
somewhere between
yesterday and tomorrow,
but no matter how
many times i count to ten
and tell you that i give up,
you don't come out—
i still can't see you.

HIDE

AND SEEK

there are four seasons
that always come back to me,
and i know i will find you
in one of them.

and i will tell her,
even if heartbreak lands
at your feet, the world
will not look at you
any differently. instead,
it will remind you that
even if love lets you go,
it doesn't mean you
aren't beautiful.

i will show her the flowers,
and when she speaks of their
beauty i will point to the clouds—
everything grows from the
things that fall and there is
nothing that the sun can't heal.

FALLING

S T A R

the sky falls
when i dream of us.

and i am made
of stars
on the inside,
just like *them*.
just like *you*.

i'm learning
how to read between the lines
and hear all of the i love yous
that were left on the tip of your
tongue.

you asked me to wait (*just a little longer*)
but i am so tired of holding my breath.

SINKING

SHIP

i built the ocean
around me (in the bathtub)
when i was five years old.
you called me a mermaid,
but i dreamt of being
the pirate.

i want you to see the whole world,
you said to me.

but i don't need both eyes to do that.
you've already shown me how
to love it with my hands.

salt-stained tears
leave me and there are
no words to stop them.

but i will swim to keep myself above water.

E Y E

OF THE STORM

there is a part of me that
will always reach out like
there is something worth
saving.

even the rain lets me
hold it before it leaves.

i will dig,
and dig,
and dig
through the wreckage
because no matter
where i find you,
you will always be
beautiful.

DIAMOND

IN THE ROUGH

my elbows are scraped
to the bone and maybe
i've bitten off more
than i can chew, but
there's nothing left to lose
except this hope buried
underneath my fingernails.

when i wash myself clean,
it still comes back.

i've grown tired of fighting
this war against my body.

beneath the skin we all look the same.

S K E L E T O N

KEY

i spend my days
leaving doors open behind me
hoping there is something you
might want to come back for;

keys on the table,
raincoat, coffee,

me.

fern.
i think it's beautiful
the way your name sounds
like it came from the wild, just like
the rest of you.

and when you asked,
can i keep you forever?

i smiled because i knew forever
wouldn't be long enough
for creatures like you & me.

BLESSING

IN DISGUISE

some days i just want
to disappear (*for a moment*)
and forget who i am—
like a sun that hides
herself behind the moon.

they watch with patient eyes,
and one day i hope they will look
at me the same.

i found the words i love you hidden in grey
skies with a chance of rain, and when you
reached out to me i showed you all of my
colours—that was the first time anyone
stopped and listened to what i had to say.

but there's something you should know.
my eyes are the size of i'm sorry, and if you
aren't sure what that means, hold on to
forgiveness a little bit longer, because i
promise, i'll need ~~to borrow~~ it soon.

i was born chasing rain(bows). there is no
storm i haven't met with an open heart,
and no matter the disaster it makes out of
me, i stay to pick up the damage with my
bare hands because it brings me closer to
the parts i need to leave behind. just like
yesterday.

i have always had trouble believing in the
future, but i love the way you say *tomorrow*
like there's so much room for us to grow.

C H A S I N G

RAINBOWS

they call me colour blind
because i love in shades of grey,
but my heart feels like sunset—
golden, steady, and always on the edge
of an ocean that keeps giving the sky
a reason to be blue.

they call me sad
because i carry storms inside my chest,
but what they don't see is that luck
has always been on my side and rain
will always be my favorite colour.

you looked like a mosaic,
so beautifully fractured
like all of your pieces were not
meant to fit.

and when you told me i should
run away *from someone like you,*
i reached out with every
part of me open—

my eyes.
these arms.
this heart.

and isn't it beautiful
the way things fall together?

you needed somewhere to land and
i wanted something to hold.

B U T T E R F L Y

EFFECT

my heart tends to live
in the wrong place at
the right time,
but i've always loved
the sound of rain
on a sunny day
and the moon after
sunrise.

i will hold the colour gold
in my hands and show you
how beautiful this life can be
even when your eyes have forgotten
how to see the light.

the sun will always find its way back to you,
just like me.

G O L D E N

H O U R

time is slipping away
and i'm worried
that when i finally wake up,
all that will be left
is a room full of memories
and a heart that lost
its way.

like love,
it will either drown you
or help you grow.

WATER

UNDER THE BRIDGE

don't spend
your time
worrying about
the bridges
they burned
when they are
already under
you.

there are moments that
understand forgiveness more
gracefully than my own—
like a garden that thrives
even after it has been picked
apart by hands that didn't
know how to hold patience.

everything is growing toward the light
and i'm still opening my eyes.

F O R G I V E

AND FORGET

i've always been the girl
looking out of car windows,
waving goodbye,
wondering how long
it will take for you
to miss me.

∴

there are pictures hanging
on the walls of this burning house and
i'm standing with my arms open
ready to catch anything that we might lose.
you grabbed my hand and said to me,

> *give it time.*
> *the smoke will rise.*

and in that moment i could feel the way
you kept me on my toes—
but i still have so far to reach.

S M O K E

A N D   M I R R O R S

these reflections keep telling me
to hate all of the things
i am meant to love.

>   i *b l i n k* my eyes
>   and start over again.

loving (myself) isn't easy,
but it always finds its way back.

there is truth hiding
underneath these pillows
like dreams resting behind
closed eyes that wanted
me to stay.

morning may leave me
with nothing to hold,
but the colour of moonrise
will visit at the same time
it did yesterday and make
constellations out of me.

you can't always see your dreams,
but that doesn't mean they aren't there.

EVERYDAY

MAGIC

you were like a magic trick
disappearing before my eyes,
but leaving me with a heart
that still believed.

i may trip over my feet
more times than i can count,
but these scrapes and bruises
remind me that my knees
were meant to touch the earth
because every climb worth knowing
begins with a prayer.

BLEEDING

HEART

my heart is a lost and found.
i keep things that others leave behind
safe in my corners
and hold on to the parts
that no one else wants to claim.
i am never empty, but i wonder
if you will ever come looking for
the things you left.

i was married once. we had a simple kind of
love, one that felt like we didn't need to try.
it was just . . . there. easy to assemble, no
directions needed, but i should have listened
when they told me that hearts built like this
are the ones that break the fastest. a little too
much use and the screws come undone and
the pieces become too hard to find.

it didn't end well. i still believe more
of my parts went missing than his, but what
heart isn't lost when it is waiting for the
end of loving someone?

i still have scarred knees from crawling
through my devastation, but somewhere
along the way i found a man who understood
my wreckage. he did not try to put me back
together, he did not try to "fix" me.

instead, he never stopped looking for me.
and now i feel the difference. sometimes,
love is meant to come undone. sometimes,
it's knowing you've found someone who will
never stop finding you.

FINDING

NEVERLAND

today i am lost,
living with my head
in the clouds.
tomorrow, i will be there,
too.

she built me up
like a mountain at sunrise
and painted my sky
with gentle hands.

and when she told me
i could be anything, i believed her
because i saw how much i could grow
with even a little of her light.

—*mama*

THE SUN

∴

WILL RISE

i will dream
of a sunrise that touches my face
and reminds me that it's okay
to be different.

*i missed you while
i was sleeping*

THE END

WITH GRATITUDE

to jarett, my home. thank you for finding me.
thank you for never letting go.

to mom, dad, larry, and family, thank you for
embracing my wild and showing me the light.
i grow because you let me.

to sam, my nocturnal heart. the dark to my
light. my laughter when i need it most. you
give my world a reason to smile.

to james and courtney, thank you for catching
my heart in midair and reminding me that
my words were meant to reach higher.

to austin, elliot, eliza, nora, delilah, and ray.
you are the most beautiful wildlings in my
life and an endless river of love, courage, and
truth. i am the youngest at heart in the
presence of you.

to zack, komal, atticus, gemma, emily, and
eva, i am forever grateful for your friendship,
strength, inspiration, and endless magic.
thank you for making my journey so much
more beautiful.

to the andrews mcmeel family, thank you for
giving my dreams a place to land.

to you, thank you for holding these words
and joining me on this path. my walk home
holds far more meaning with you here.

Andrews McMeel Publishing
a division of Andrews McMeel Universal
1130 Walnut Street, Kansas City, Missouri 64106

www.andrewsmcmeel.com

19 20 21 22 23 RR2 10 9 8 7 6 5 4 3 2 1

ISBN: 978-1-5248-5096-8

Library of Congress Control Number:
2019930115

Editor: Patty Rice
Designer/Art Director: Julie Barnes and wilder
Production Editor: Dave Shaw
Production Manager: Cliff Koehler

ATTENTION: SCHOOLS AND BUSINESSES
Andrews McMeel books are available at quantity
discounts with bulk purchase for educational,
business, or sales promotional use. For information,
please e-mail the Andrews McMeel Publishing
Special Sales Department:
specialsales@amuniversal.com.

wilderpoetry.com

follow the visual story on instagram:
wilderpoetry